TED HUGHES

Crow

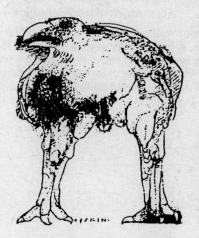

From the Life and Songs
of the Crow

faber and faber
LONDON · BOSTON

First published in 1972
by Faber and Faber Limited
3 Queen Square London WC1N 3AU
First published in Faber Paperback 1974
Reprinted 1976, 1981, 1985 and 1986

Printed in Great Britain by
Whitstable Litho Ltd.
Whitstable, Kent
All rights reserved

© Ted Hughes 1970, 1972
Grateful acknowledgement is made to the
Abraham Woursell Foundation

ISBN 0-571-09915-7

In Memory
of Assia and Shura

Contents

8

Publisher's Note

This new edition of CROW contains seven new poems which did not appear in the original edition. They are:

Two Legends

I

Black was the without eye
Black the within tongue
Black was the heart
Black the liver, black the lungs
Unable to suck in light
Black the blood in its loud tunnel
Black the bowels packed in furnace
Black too the muscles
Striving to pull out into the light
Black the nerves, black the brain
With its tombed visions
Black also the soul, the huge stammer
Of the cry that, swelling, could not
Pronounce its sun.

II

Black is the wet otter's head, lifted.
Black is the rock, plunging in foam.
Black is the gall lying on the bed of the blood.

Black is the earth-globe, one inch under,
An egg of blackness
Where sun and moon alternate their weathers

To hatch a crow, a black rainbow
Bent in emptiness
                     over emptiness

But flying

Lineage

In the beginning was Scream
Who begat Blood
Who begat Eye
Who begat Fear
Who begat Wing
Who begat Bone
Who begat Granite
Who begat Violet
Who begat Guitar
Who begat Sweat
Who begat Adam
Who begat Mary
Who begat God
Who begat Nothing
Who begat Never
Never Never Never

Who begat Crow

Screaming for Blood
Grubs, crusts
Anything

Trembling featherless elbows in the nest's filth

Examination at the Womb-door

Who owns these scrawny little feet?   *Death*.
Who owns this bristly scorched-looking face?   *Death*.
Who owns these still-working lungs?   *Death*.
Who owns this utility coat of muscles?   *Death*.
Who owns these unspeakable guts?   *Death*.
Who owns these questionable brains?   *Death*.
All this messy blood?   *Death*.
These minimum-efficiency eyes?   *Death*.
This wicked little tongue?   *Death*.
This occasional wakefulness?   *Death*.

Given, stolen, or held pending trial?
Held.

Who owns the whole rainy, stony earth?   *Death*.
Who owns all of space?   *Death*.

Who is stronger than hope?   *Death*.
Who is stronger than the will?   *Death*.
Stronger than love?   *Death*.
Stronger than life?   *Death*.

But who is stronger than death?
                              Me, evidently.

Pass, Crow.

A Kill

Flogged lame with legs
Shot through the head with balled brains
Shot blind with eyes
Nailed down by his own ribs
Strangled just short of his last gasp
By his own windpipe
Clubbed unconscious by his own heart

Seeing his life stab through him, a dream flash
As he drowned in his own blood

Dragged under by the weight of his guts

Uttering a bowel-emptying cry which was his roots tearing
out
Of the bedrock atom
Gaping his mouth and letting the cry rip through him as at a
distance

And smashed into the rubbish of the ground

He managed to hear, faint and far—'It's a boy!'

Then everything went black

Crow and Mama

When Crow cried his mother's ear
Scorched to a stump.

When he laughed she wept
Blood her breasts her palms her brow all wept blood.

He tried a step, then a step, and again a step—
Every one scarred her face for ever.

When he burst out in rage
She fell back with an awful gash and a fearful cry.

When he stopped she closed on him like a book
On a bookmark, he had to get going.

He jumped into the car the towrope
Was around her neck he jumped out.

He jumped into the plane but her body was jammed in the
                                                    jet—
There was a great row, the flight was cancelled.

He jumped into the rocket and its trajectory
Drilled clean through her heart he kept on

And it was cosy in the rocket, he could not see much
But he peered out through the portholes at Creation

And saw the stars millions of miles away
And saw the future and the universe

Opening and opening
And kept on and slept and at last

Crashed on the moon awoke and crawled out

Under his mother's buttocks.

The Door

Out under the sun stands a body.
It is growth of the solid world.

It is part of the world's earthen wall.
The earth's plants—such as the genitals
And the flowerless navel
Live in its crevices.
Also, some of earth's creatures—such as the mouth.
All are rooted in earth, or eat earth, earthy,
Thickening the wall.

Only there is a doorway in the wall—
A black doorway:
The eye's pupil.

Through that doorway came Crow.

Flying from sun to sun, he found this home.

A Childish Prank

Man's and woman's bodies lay without souls,
Dully gaping, foolishly staring, inert
On the flowers of Eden.
God pondered.

The problem was so great, it dragged him asleep.

Crow laughed.
He bit the Worm, God's only son,
Into two writhing halves.

He stuffed into man the tail half
With the wounded end hanging out.

He stuffed the head half headfirst into woman
And it crept in deeper and up
To peer out through her eyes
Calling its tail-half to join up quickly, quickly
Because O it was painful.

Man awoke being dragged across the grass.
Woman awoke to see him coming.
Neither knew what had happened.

God went on sleeping.

Crow went on laughing.

Crow's First Lesson

God tried to teach Crow how to talk.
'Love,' said God. 'Say, Love.'
Crow gaped, and the white shark crashed into the sea
And went rolling downwards, discovering its own depth.

'No, no,' said God, 'Say Love. Now try it. LOVE.'
Crow gaped, and a bluefly, a tsetse, a mosquito
Zoomed out and down
To their sundry flesh-pots.

'A final try,' said God. 'Now, LOVE.'
Crow convulsed, gaped, retched and
Man's bodiless prodigious head
Bulbed out onto the earth, with swivelling eyes,
Jabbering protest—

And Crow retched again, before God could stop him.
And woman's vulva dropped over man's neck and tightened.
The two struggled together on the grass.
God struggled to part them, cursed, wept—

Crow flew guiltily off.

Crow Alights

Crow saw the herded mountains, steaming in the morning.
And he saw the sea
Dark-spined, with the whole earth in its coils.
He saw the stars, fuming away into the black, mushrooms of
   the nothing forest, clouding their spores, the virus of God.

And he shivered with the horror of Creation.

In the hallucination of the horror
He saw this shoe, with no sole, rain-sodden,
Lying on a moor.
And there was this garbage can, bottom rusted away,
A playing place for the wind, in a waste of puddles.

There was this coat, in the dark cupboard, in the silent room,
                                  in the silent house.
There was this face, smoking its cigarette between the dusk
                        window and the fire's embers.

Near the face, this hand, motionless.

Near the hand, this cup.

Crow blinked.   He blinked.   Nothing faded.

He stared at the evidence.

Nothing escaped him. (Nothing could escape.)

That Moment

When the pistol muzzle oozing blue vapour
Was lifted away
Like a cigarette lifted from an ashtray

And the only face left in the world
Lay broken
Between hands that relaxed, being too late

And the trees closed forever
And the streets closed forever

And the body lay on the gravel
Of the abandoned world
Among abandoned utilities
Exposed to infinity forever

Crow had to start searching for something to eat.

Crow Hears Fate Knock on the Door

Crow looked at the world, mountainously heaped.
He looked at the heavens, littering away
Beyond every limit.
He looked in front of his feet at the little stream
Chugging on like an auxiliary motor
Fastened to this infinite engine.

He imagined the whole engineering
Of its assembly, repairs and maintenance—
And felt helpless.

He plucked grass-heads and gazed into them
Waiting for first instructions.
He studied a stone from the stream.
He found a dead mole and slowly he took it apart
Then stared at the gobbets, feeling helpless.
He walked, he walked
Letting the translucent starry spaces
Blow in his ear cluelessly.

Yet the prophecy inside him, like a grimace,
Was I WILL MEASURE IT ALL AND OWN IT ALL
AND I WILL BE INSIDE IT
AS INSIDE MY OWN LAUGHTER
AND NOT STARING OUT AT IT THROUGH WALLS
OF MY EYE'S COLD QUARANTINE
FROM A BURIED CELL OF BLOODY BLACKNESS—

This prophecy was inside him, like a steel spring

Slowly rending the vital fibres.

Crow Tyrannosaurus

Creation quaked voices—
It was a cortege
Of mourning and lament
Crow could hear and he looked around fearfully.

The swift's body fled past
Pulsating
With insects
And their anguish, all it had eaten.

The cat's body writhed
Gagging
A tunnel
Of incoming death-struggles, sorrow on sorrow.

And the dog was a bulging filterbag
Of all the deaths it had gulped for the flesh and the bones.
It could not digest their screeching finales.
Its shapeless cry was a blort of all those voices.

Even man he was a walking
Abattoir
Of innocents—
His brain incinerating their outcry.

Crow thought 'Alas
Alas ought I
To stop eating
And try to become the light?'

But his eye saw a grub. And his head, trapsprung, stabbed.
And he listened

And he heard
Weeping

Grubs   grubs   He stabbed   he stabbed
Weeping
Weeping

Weeping he walked and stabbed

Thus came the eye's
                    roundness
                              the ear's
                                    deafness.

Crow's Account of the Battle

There was this terrific battle.
The noise was as much
As the limits of possible noise could take.
There were screams higher groans deeper
Than any ear could hold.
Many eardrums burst and some walls
Collapsed to escape the noise.
Everything struggled on its way
Through this tearing deafness
As through a torrent in a dark cave.

The cartridges were banging off, as planned,
The fingers were keeping things going
According to excitement and orders.
The unhurt eyes were full of deadliness.
The bullets pursued their courses
Through clods of stone, earth and skin,
Through intestines, pocket-books, brains, hair, teeth
According to Universal laws.
And mouths cried 'Mamma'
From sudden traps of calculus,
Theorems wrenched men in two,
Shock-severed eyes watched blood
Squandering as from a drain-pipe
Into the blanks between stars.
Faces slammed down into clay
As for the making of a life-mask
Knew that even on the sun's surface.
They could not be learning more or more to the point.
Reality was giving its lesson,
Its mishmash of scripture and physics,
With here, brains in hands, for example,
And there, legs in a treetop.

There was no escape except into death.
And still it went on—it outlasted
Many prayers, many a proved watch,
Many bodies in excellent trim,
Till the explosives ran out
And sheer weariness supervened
And what was left looked round at what was left.

Then everybody wept,
Or sat, too exhausted to weep,
Or lay, too hurt to weep.
And when the smoke cleared it became clear
This had happened too often before
And was going to happen too often in future
And happened too easily
Bones were too like lath and twigs
Blood was too like water
Cries were too like silence
The most terrible grimaces too like footprints in mud
And shooting somebody through the midriff
Was too like striking a match
Too like potting a snooker ball
Too like tearing up a bill
Blasting the whole world to bits
Was too like slamming a door
Too like dropping in a chair
Exhausted with rage
Too like being blown to bits yourself
Which happened too easily
With too like no consequences.

So the survivors stayed.
And the earth and the sky stayed.
Everything took the blame.

Not a leaf flinched, nobody smiled.

The Black Beast

Where is the Black Beast?
Crow, like an owl, swivelled his head.
Where is the Black Beast?
Crow hid in its bed, to ambush it.
Where is the Black Beast?
Crow sat in its chair, telling loud lies against the Black Beast.
Where is it?
Crow shouted after midnight, pounding the wall with a last.
Where is the Black Beast?
Crow split his enemy's skull to the pineal gland.
Where is the Black Beast?
Crow crucified a frog under a microscope, he peered into the
                                        brain of a dogfish.
Where is the Black Beast?
Crow killed his brother and turned him inside out to stare at
                                        his colour.
Where is the Black Beast?
Crow roasted the earth to a clinker, he charged into space—
Where is the Black Beast?
The silences of space decamped, space flitted in every
                                        direction—
Where is the Black Beast?
Crow flailed immensely through the vacuum, he screeched
                                after the disappearing stars—
Where is it? Where is the Black Beast?

A Grin

There was this hidden grin.
It wanted a permanent home. It tried faces
In their forgetful moments, the face for instance
Of a woman pushing a baby out between her legs
But that didn't last long the face
Of a man so preoccupied
With the flying steel in the instant
Of the car-crash he left his face
To itself that was even shorter, the face
Of a machine-gunner a long burst not long enough and
The face of a steeplejack the second
Before he hit the paving, the faces
Of two lovers in the seconds
They got so far into each other they forgot
Each other completely that was O.K.
But none of it lasted.

So the grin tried the face
Of somebody lost in sobbing
A murderer's face and the racking moments
Of the man smashing everything
He could reach and had strength to smash
Before he went beyond his body.

It tried the face
In the electric chair to get a tenure
In eternal death, but that too relaxed.

The grin
Sank back, temporarily nonplussed,
Into the skull.

Crow Communes

'Well,' said Crow, 'What first?'
God, exhausted with Creation, snored.
'Which way?' said Crow, 'Which way first?'
God's shoulder was the mountain on which Crow sat.
'Come,' said Crow, 'Let's discuss the situation.'
God lay, agape, a great carcase.

Crow tore off a mouthful and swallowed.

'Will this cipher divulge itself to digestion
Under hearing beyond understanding?'

(That was the first jest.)

Yet, it's true, he suddenly felt much stronger.

Crow, the hierophant, humped, impenetrable.

Half-illumined. Speechless.

(Appalled.)

Crow's Account of St George

He sees everything in the Universe
Is a track of numbers racing towards an answer.
With delirious joy, with nimble balance
He rides those racing tracks. He makes a silence.
He refrigerates an emptiness,
Decreates all to outer space,
Then unpicks numbers. The great stones fall open.
With the faintest breath
He melts cephalopods and sorts raw numbers
Out of their dregs. With tweezers of number
He picks the gluey heart out of an inaudibly squeaking cell—
He hears something. He turns—
A demon, dripping ordure, is grinning in the doorway.
It vanishes. He concentrates—
With a knife-edge of numbers
He cuts the heart cleanly in two. He shivers—
Looks up. A demon with a face flat as a snail
Or the underface of a shark, is grinning at him
Through the window. It vanishes. Confused,
Shaken, he aims his attention—
Finding the core of the heart is a nest of numbers.
His heart begins to pound, his hand trembles.
Something grabs at his arm. He turns. A bird-head,
Bald, lizard-eyed, the size of a football, on two staggering
                                                            bird-legs

Gapes at him all the seams and pleats of its throat,
Clutching at the carpet with horny feet,
Threatens. He lifts a chair—fear lifts him—
He smashes the egg-shell object to a blood-rag,
A lumping sprawl, he tramples the bubbling mess.
The shark-face is screaming in the doorway
Opening its fangs. The chair again—

He splits that face and beats the chair to pieces
On the writhing unbreakably tough horror
Till it lies still. Now with a shriek
An object four times bigger than the others—
A belly-ball of hair, with crab-legs, eyeless,
Jabs its pincers into his face,
Its belly opens—a horrible oven of fangs,
The claws are clawing to drag him towards it.
He snatches from its mount on the wall a sword,
A ceremonial Japanese decapitator,
And as hacking a path through thicket he scatters
The lopped segments, the opposition collapses.
He stands trousered in blood and log-splits
The lolling body, bifurcates it
Top to bottom, kicks away the entrails—
Steps out of the blood-wallow. Recovers—

Drops the sword and runs dumb-faced from the house
Where his wife and children lie in their blood.

A Disaster

There came news of a word.
Crow saw it killing men. He ate well.
He saw it bulldozing
Whole cities to rubble. Again he ate well.
He saw its excreta poisoning seas.
He became watchful.
He saw its breath burning whole lands
To dusty char.
He flew clear and peered.

The word oozed its way, all mouth,
Earless, eyeless.
He saw it sucking the cities
Like the nipples of a sow
Drinking out all the people
Till there were none left,
All digested inside the word.

Ravenous, the word tried its great lips
On the earth's bulge, like a giant lamprey—
There it started to suck.

But its effort weakened.
It could digest nothing but people.
So there it shrank, wrinkling weaker,
Puddling
Like a collapsing mushroom.
Finally, a drying salty lake.
Its era was over.
All that remained of it a brittle desert
Dazzling with the bones of earth's people

Where Crow walked and mused.

The Battle of Osfrontalis

Words came with Life Insurance policies—
Crow feigned dead.
Words came with warrants to conscript him—
Crow feigned mad.
Words came with blank cheques—
He drew Minnie Mice on them.
Words came with Aladdin's lamp—
He sold it and bought a pie.
Words came in the likeness of vaginas in a row—
He called in his friends.
Words came in the likeness of a wreathed vagina pouring out
                                                    Handel—
He gave it to the museum.
Words came with barrels of wine—
He let them go sour and pickled his onions.

Crow whistled.

Words attacked him with the glottal bomb—
He wasn't listening.
Words surrounded and over-ran him with light aspirates—
He was dozing.
Words infiltrated guerrilla labials—
Crow clapped his beak, scratched it.
Words swamped him with consonantal masses—
Crow took a sip of water and thanked heaven.

Words retreated, suddenly afraid
Into the skull of a dead jester
Taking the whole world with them—

But the world did not notice.

And Crow yawned—long ago
He had picked that skull empty.

Crow's Theology

Crow realized God loved him—
Otherwise, he would have dropped dead.
So that was proved.
Crow reclined, marvelling, on his heart-beat.

And he realized that God spoke Crow—
Just existing was His revelation.

But what
Loved the stones and spoke stone?
They seemed to exist too.
And what spoke that strange silence
After his clamour of caws faded?

And what loved the shot-pellets
That dribbled from those strung-up mummifying crows?
What spoke the silence of lead?

Crow realized there were two Gods—

One of them much bigger than the other
Loving his enemies
And having all the weapons.

Crow's Fall

When Crow was white he decided the sun was too white.
He decided it glared much too whitely.
He decided to attack it and defeat it.

He got his strength flush and in full glitter.
He clawed and fluffed his rage up.
He aimed his beak direct at the sun's centre.

He laughed himself to the centre of himself

And attacked.

At his battle cry trees grew suddenly old,
Shadows flattened.

But the sun brightened—
It brightened, and Crow returned charred black.

He opened his mouth but what came out was charred black.

'Up there', he managed,
'Where white is black and black is white, I won.'

Crow and the Birds

When the eagle soared clear through a dawn distilling of
                                    emerald
When the curlew trawled in seadusk through a chime of
                                  wineglasses
When the swallow swooped through a woman's song in a
                                  cavern
And the swift flicked through the breath of a violet

When the owl sailed clear of tomorrow's conscience
And the sparrow preened himself of yesterday's promise
And the heron laboured clear of the Bessemer upglare
And the bluetit zipped clear of lace panties
And the woodpecker drummed clear of the rotovator and the
                                  rose-farm
And the peewit tumbled clear of the laundromat

While the bullfinch plumped in the apple bud
And the goldfinch bulbed in the sun
And the wryneck crooked in the moon
And the dipper peered from the dewball

Crow spraddled head-down in the beach-garbage, guzzling a
                                  dropped ice-cream.

Criminal Ballad

There was a man and when he was born
A woman fell between the ship and the jetty
At a heave from the moon and the sun
Her pleading cries were humbled out
And when he sucked
And fastened greedily at the hot supply
An old lady's head sank sideways, her lips relaxed
Drained of fuel, she became a mere mask
Reflected in half-empty brown bottles
And the eyes of relatives
That were little circles in blind skin
And when he ran and got his toy squealing with delight
An old man pulled from under the crush of metal
Gazed towards the nearby polished shoes
And slowly forgot the deaths in Homer
The sparrowfall natural economy
Of the dark simple curtain
And when he clasped his first love belly to belly
The yellow woman started to bellow
On the floor, and the husband stared
Through an anaesthetized mask
And felt the cardboard of his body
And when he walked in his garden and saw his children
Bouncing among the dogs and balls
He could not hear their silly songs and the barking
For machine guns
And a screaming and laughing in the cell
Which had got tangled in the air with his hearing
And he could not turn towards the house
Because the woman of complete pain rolling in flame
Was calling to him all the time
From the empty goldfish pond

And when he began to shout to defend his hearing
And shake his vision to splinters
His hands covered with blood suddenly
And now he ran from the children and ran through the house
Holding his bloody hands clear of everything
And ran along the road and into the wood
And under the leaves he sat weeping

And under the leaves he sat weeping

Till he began to laugh

Crow on the Beach

Hearing shingle explode, seeing it skip,
Crow sucked his tongue.
Seeing sea-grey mash a mountain of itself
Crow tightened his goose-pimples.
Feeling spray from the sea's root nothinged on his crest
Crow's toes gripped the wet pebbles.
When the smell of the whale's den, the gulfing of the crab's
                                                    last prayer,

Gimletted in his nostril
He grasped he was on earth.
                              He knew he grasped
Something fleeting
Of the sea's ogreish outcry and convulsion.
He knew he was the wrong listener unwanted
To understand or help—

His utmost gaping of brain in his tiny skull
Was just enough to wonder, about the sea,

What could be hurting so much?

The Contender

There was this man and he was the strongest
Of the strong.
He gritted his teeth like a cliff.
Though his body was sweeling away like a torrent on a cliff
Smoking towards dark gorges
There he nailed himself with nails of nothing

All the women in the world could not move him
They came their mouths deformed against stone
They came and their tears salted his nail-holes
Only adding their embitterment
To his effort
He abandoned his grin to them his grimace
In his face upwards body he lay face downwards
As a dead man adamant

His sandals could not move him they burst their thongs
And rotted from his fixture
All the men in the world could not move him
They wore at him with their shadows and little sounds
Their arguments were a relief
Like heather flowers
His belt could not endure the siege—it burst
And lay broken
He grinned
Little children came in chorus to move him
But he glanced at them out of his eye-corners
Over the edge of his grin
And they lost their courage for life

Oak forests came and went with the hawk's wing
Mountains rose and fell
He lay crucified with all his strength
On the earth
Grinning towards the sun
Through the tiny holes of his eyes
And towards the moon
And towards the whole paraphernalia of the heavens
Through the seams of his face
With the strings of his lips
Grinning through his atoms and decay
Grinning into the black
Into the ringing nothing
Through the bones of his teeth

Sometimes with eyes closed

In his senseless trial of strength.

Oedipus Crow

Mummies stormed his torn insides
With their bandages and embalming honey.
He contorted clear, he vomited empty—
He flew.

A gravestone fell on his foot
And took root—
He bit through the bone and he fled.

The water-spirit in the happy valley
Twined his brains with primroses, dogroses,
Pulling his mouth down to the wet humus—
With a howl he left what she held.

And he ran, cheered by the sound of his foot and its echo
And by the watch on his wrist

One-legged, gutless and brainless, the rag of himself—

So Death tripped him easy
And held him up with a laugh, only just alive.

And his watch galloped away in a cloud of corpse-dust.

Crow dangled from his one claw—corrected.

A warning.

Crow's Vanity

Looking close in the evil mirror Crow saw
Mistings of civilizations   towers   gardens
Battles he wiped the glass   but there came

Mistings of skyscrapers   webs of cities
Steaming the glass he wiped it   there came

Spread of swampferns fronded on the mistings
A trickling spider   he wiped the glass   he peered

For a glimpse of the usual grinning face

But it was no good he was breathing too heavy
And too hot   and space was too cold

And here came the misty ballerinas
The burning gulfs   the hanging gardens   it was eerie

A Horrible Religious Error

When the serpent emerged, earth-bowel brown,
From the hatched atom
With its alibi self twisted around it

Lifting a long neck
And balancing that deaf and mineral stare
The sphinx of the final fact

And flexing on that double flameflicker tongue
A syllable like the rustling of the spheres

God's grimace writhed, a leaf in the furnace

And man's and woman's knees melted, they collapsed
Their neck-muscles melted, their brows bumped the ground
Their tears evacuated visibly
They whispered 'Your will is our peace.'

But Crow only peered.
                        Then took a step or two forward,
Grabbed this creature by the slackskin nape,

Beat the hell out of it, and ate it.

Crow Tries the Media

He wanted to sing about her

He didn't want comparisons with the earth or anything to do
with it

Oversold like detergents
He did not even want words
Waving their long tails in public
With their prostitute's exclamations

He wanted to sing very clear

But this tank had been parked on his voice
And his throat was nipped between the Roman Emperor's
finger and thumb

Like the neck of a linnet
While King Kong in person
Held the loop of his blood like a garotte
And tycoons gambled his glands away in a fog of cigar smoke

He shuddered out of himself he got so naked
When he touched her breast it hurt him

He wanted to sing to her soul simply

But still Manhattan weighed on his eyelid

He looked at the corner of her eye
His tongue moved like a poisoned estuary

He touched the smiling corner of her mouth
His voice reverberated like the slow millstone of London
Raising a filthy haze,
her shape dimmed.

Crow's Nerve Fails

Crow, feeling his brain slip,
Finds his every feather the fossil of a murder.

Who murdered all these?
These living dead, that root in his nerves and his blood
Till he is visibly black?

How can he fly from his feathers?
And why have they homed on him?

Is he the archive of their accusations?
Or their ghostly purpose, their pining vengeance?
Or their unforgiven prisoner?

He cannot be forgiven.

His prison is the earth. Clothed in his conviction,
Trying to remember his crimes

Heavily he flies.

In Laughter

Cars collide and erupt luggage and babies
In laughter
The steamer upends and goes under saluting like a stuntman
In laughter
The nosediving aircraft concludes with a boom
In laughter
People's arms and legs fly off and fly on again
In laughter
The haggard mask on the bed rediscovers its pang
In laughter, in laughter
The meteorite crashes
With extraordinarily ill-luck on the pram

The ears and eyes are bundled up
Are folded up in the hair,
Wrapped in the carpet, the wallpaper, tied with the lampflex
Only the teeth work on
And the heart, dancing on in its open cave
Helpless on the strings of laughter

While the tears are nickel-plated and come through doors
                                                with a bang

And the wails stun with fear
And the bones
Jump from the torment flesh has to stay for

Stagger some distance and fall in full view

Still laughter scampers around on centipede boots
Still it runs all over on caterpillar tread
And rolls back onto the mattress, legs in the air

But it's only human

And finally it's had enough—enough!
And slowly sits up, exhausted,
And slowly starts to fasten buttons,
With long pauses,

Like somebody the police have come for.

Crow Frowns

Is he his own strength?
What is its signature?
Or is he a key, cold-feeling
To the fingers of prayer?

He is a prayer-wheel, his heart hums.
His eating is the wind—
Its patient power of appeal.
His footprints assail infinity

With signatures: We are here, we are here.
He is the long waiting for something
To use him for some everything
Having so carefully made him

Of nothing.

Magical Dangers

Crow thought of a palace—
Its lintel crashed on him, his bones were found.

Crow thought of a fast car—
It plucked his spine out, and left him empty and armless.

Crow thought of the wind's freedom—
And his eyes evaporated, the wind whistled over the Turkish
Saddle.

Crow thought of a wage—
And it choked him, it was cut unspoiled from his dead
stomach.

Crow thought of the soft and warm that is long remembered—
It blindfolded him with silk, it gangplanked him into a
volcano.

Crow thought of intelligence—
It turned the key against him and he tore at its fruitless bars.

Crow thought of nature's stupor—
And an oak tree grew out of his ear.

A row of his black children sat in the top.
They flew off.

Crow
Never again moved.

Robin Song

I am the hunted king
  Of the frost and big icicles
    And the bogey cold
    With its wind boots.

I am the uncrowned
  Of the rainworld
    Hunted by lightning and thunder
    And rivers.

I am the lost child
  Of the wind
    Who goes through me looking for something else
    Who can't recognize me though I cry.

I am the maker
  Of the world
    That rolls to crush
    And silence my knowledge.

Conjuring in Heaven

So finally there was nothing.
It was put inside nothing.
Nothing was added to it
And to prove it didn't exist
Squashed flat as nothing with nothing.

Chopped up with a nothing
Shaken in a nothing
Turned completely inside out
And scattered over nothing—
So everybody saw that it was nothing
And that nothing more could be done with it

And so it was dropped. Prolonged applause in Heaven.

It hit the ground and broke open—

There lay Crow, cataleptic.

Crow Goes Hunting

Crow
Decided to try words.

He imagined some words for the job, a lovely pack—
Clear-eyed, resounding, well-trained,
With strong teeth.
You could not find a better bred lot.

He pointed out the hare and away went the words
Resounding.
Crow was Crow without fail, but what is a hare?

It converted itself to a concrete bunker.
The words circled protesting, resounding.

Crow turned the words into bombs—they blasted the bunker.
The bits of bunker flew up—a flock of starlings.

Crow turned the words into shotguns, they shot down the
                                                    starlings.
The falling starlings turned to a cloudburst.

Crow turned the words into a reservoir, collecting the water.
The water turned into an earthquake, swallowing the
                                                    reservoir.

The earthquake turned into a hare and leaped for the hill
Having eaten Crow's words.

Crow gazed after the bounding hare
Speechless with admiration.

Owl's Song

He sang
How the swan blanched forever
How the wolf threw away its telltale heart
And the stars dropped their pretence
The air gave up appearances
Water went deliberately numb
The rock surrendered its last hope
And cold died beyond knowledge

He sang
How everything had nothing more to lose

Then sat still with fear

Seeing the clawtrack of star
Hearing the wingbeat of rock

And his own singing

Crow's Undersong

She cannot come all the way

She comes as far as water no further

She comes with the birth push
Into eyelashes into nipples the fingertips
She comes as far as blood and to the tips of hair
She comes to the fringe of voice
She stays
Even after life even among the bones

She comes singing she cannot manage an instrument
She comes too cold afraid of clothes
And too slow with eyes wincing frightened
When she looks into wheels

She comes sluttish she cannot keep house
She can just keep clean
She cannot count she cannot last

She comes dumb she cannot manage words
She brings petals in their nectar fruits in their plush
She brings a cloak of feathers an animal rainbow
She brings her favourite furs and these are her speeches

She has come amorous it is all she has come for

If there had been no hope she would not have come

And there would have been no crying in the city

(There would have been no city)

Crow's Elephant Totem Song

Once upon a time
God made this Elephant.
Then it was delicate and small
It was not freakish at all
Or melancholy

The Hyenas sang in the scrub: You are beautiful—
They showed their scorched heads and grinning expressions
Like the half-rotted stumps of amputations—
We envy your grace
Waltzing through the thorny growth
O take us with you to the Land of Peaceful
O ageless eyes of innocence and kindliness
Lift us from the furnaces
And furies of our blackened faces
Within these hells we writhe
Shut in behind the bars of our teeth
In hourly battle with a death
The size of the earth
Having the strength of the earth.

So the Hyenas ran under the Elephant's tail
As like a lithe and rubber oval
He strolled gladly around inside his ease
But he was not God no it was not his
To correct the damned
In rage in madness then they lit their mouths
They tore out his entrails
They divided him among their several hells
To cry all his separate pieces
Swallowed and inflamed
Amidst paradings of infernal laughter.

At the Resurrection
The Elephant got himself together with correction
Deadfall feet and toothproof body and bulldozing bones
And completely altered brains
Behind aged eyes, that were wicked and wise.

So through the orange blaze and blue shadow
Of the afterlife, effortless and immense,
The Elephant goes his own way, a walking sixth sense,
And opposite and parallel
The sleepless Hyenas go
Along a leafless skyline trembling like an oven roof
With a whipped run
Their shame-flags tucked hard down
Over the gutsacks
Crammed with putrefying laughter
Blotched black with the leakage and seepings
And they sing: 'Ours is the land
Of loveliness and beautiful
Is the putrid mouth of the leopard
And the graves of fever
Because it is all we have—'
And they vomit their laughter.

And the Elephant sings deep in the forest-maze
About a star of deathless and painless peace
But no astronomer can find where it is.

Dawn's Rose

Is melting an old frost moon.

Agony under agony, the quiet of dust,
And a crow talking to stony skylines.

Desolate is the crow's puckered cry
As an old woman's mouth
When the eyelids have finished
And the hills continue.

A cry
Wordless
As the newborn baby's grieving
On the steely scales.

As the dull gunshot and its after-râle
Among conifers, in rainy twilight.

Or the suddenly dropped, heavily dropped
Star of blood on the fat leaf.

Crow's Playmates

Lonely Crow created the gods for playmates—
But the mountain god tore free

And Crow fell back from the wall-face of mountains
By which he was so much lessened.

The river-god subtracted the rivers
From his living liquids.

God after god—and each tore from him
Its lodging place and its power.

Crow straggled, limply bedraggled his remnant.
He was his own leftover, the spat-out scrag.

He was what his brain could make nothing of.

So the least, least-living object extant
Wandered over his deathless greatness

Lonelier than ever.

Crowego

Crow followed Ulysses till he turned
As a worm, which Crow ate.

Grappling with Hercules' two puff-adders
He strangled in error Dejanira.

The gold melted out of Hercules' ashes
Is an electrode in Crow's brain.

Drinking Beowulf's blood, and wrapped in his hide,
Crow communes with poltergeists out of old ponds.

His wings are the stiff back of his only book,
Himself the only page—of solid ink.

So he gazes into the quag of the past
Like a gypsy into the crystal of the future,

Like a leopard into a fat land.

The Smile

Began under the groan of the oldest forest
It ran through the clouds, a third light
And it ran through the skin of the earth

It came circling the earth
Like the lifted bow
Of a wave's submarine running
Tossing the willows, and swelling the elm-tops
Looking for its occasion

But people were prepared
They met it
With visor smiles, mirrors of ricochet
With smiles that stole a bone
And smiles that went off with a mouthful of blood
And smiles that left poison in a numb place
Or doubled up
Covering a getaway

But the smile was too vast, it outflanked all
It was too tiny it slipped between the atoms
So that the steel screeched open
Like a gutted rabbit, the skin was nothing
Then the pavement and the air and the light
Confined all the jumping blood
No better than a paper bag
People were running with bandages
But the world was a draughty gap
The whole creation
Was just a broken gutter pipe

And there was the unlucky person's eye
Pinned under its brow
Widening for the darkness behind it
Which kept right on getting wider, darker
As if the soul were not working

And at that very moment the smile arrived

And the crowd, shoving to get a glimpse of a man's soul
Stripped to its last shame,
Met this smile
That rose through his torn roots
Touching his lips, altering his eyes
And for a moment
Mending everything

Before it swept out and away across the earth.

Crow Improvises

There was this man
Who took the sun in one hand, a leaf in the other—
The spark that jumped burned out his name.
So he took his lavender-bag ancestors under one arm
And his twisting dog under the other—
The spark that flash-thumped fused his watch of all things,
And left a black orifice instead of a time-sense.
So he took the battle of the Somme in one hand
And a sleeping tablet in the other—
The spark that blasted blew the valves of his laugh.
So he took the humane-killed skull of a horse in one hand
And a baby's fairy-bait molar in the other—
The spark that banged burned out his weeper.
So he leaned one hand on a gravestone
With his jolly roger in the other—
The spark that clouted cloaked him all in Iguana.
So he rested a dead vole in one hand
And grasped Relativity in the other—
The spark that gored through gouged out his wordage.
So in one hand he caught a girl's laugh—all there was of it,
In the other a seven-year honeymoon—all that he
                                         remembered—
The spark that crashed through coked up his gonads.
So in one hand he held a sham-dead spider,
With the other he reached for the bible—
The spark that thunderbolted blanched his every whisker.

So he took his birth-sneeze in one hand
And his death-chill in the other
And let the spark scour him to ashes.

And so the smile not even Leonardo

Could have fathomed
Flew off into the air, the rubbish heap of laughter
Screams, discretions, indiscretions etcetera

Crowcolour

Crow was so much blacker
Than the moon's shadow
He had stars.

He was as much blacker
Than any negro
As a negro's eye-pupil.

Even, like the sun,
Blacker
Than any blindness.

Crow's Battle Fury

When the patient, shining with pain,
Suddenly pales,
Crow makes a noise suspiciously like laughter.

Seeing the night-city, on the earth's blue bulge,
Trembling its tambourine,
He bellows laughter till the tears come.

Remembering the painted masks and the looming of the
balloons
Of the pinpricked dead
He rolls on the ground helpless.

And he sees his remote feet and he chokes he
Holds his aching sides—
He can hardly bear it.

One of his eyes sinks into his skull, tiny as a pin,
One opens, a gaping dish of pupils,
His temple-veins gnarl, each like the pulsing head of a month-
old baby,
His heels double to the front,
His lips lift off his cheekbone, his heart and his liver fly in his
throat,
Blood blasts from the crown of his head in a column—

Such as cannot be in this world.

A hair's breadth out of the world

(With his glared off face glued back into position
A dead man's eyes plugged back into his sockets

A dead man's heart screwed in under his ribs
His tattered guts stitched back into position
His shattered brains covered with a steel cowl)

He comes forward a step,
                    and a step,
                              and a step—

Crow Blacker than ever

When God, disgusted with man,
Turned towards heaven.
And man, disgusted with God,
Turned towards Eve,
Things looked like falling apart.

But Crow   Crow
Crow nailed them together,
Nailing Heaven and earth together—

So man cried, but with God's voice.
And God bled, but with man's blood.

Then heaven and earth creaked at the joint
Which became gangrenous and stank—
A horror beyond redemption.

The agony did not diminish.

Man could not be man nor God God.

The agony

Grew.

Crow

Grinned

Crying: 'This is my Creation,'

Flying the black flag of himself.

Revenge Fable

There was a person
Could not get rid of his mother
As if he were her topmost twig.
So he pounded and hacked at her
With numbers and equations and laws
Which he invented and called truth.
He investigated, incriminated
And penalized her, like Tolstoy,
Forbidding, screaming and condemning,
Going for her with a knife,
Obliterating her with disgusts
Bulldozers and detergents
Requisitions and central heating
Rifles and whisky and bored sleep.

With all her babes in her arms, in ghostly weepings,
She died.

His head fell off like a leaf.

A Bedtime Story

Once upon a time there was a person
Almost a person

Somehow he could not quite see
Somehow he could not quite hear
He could not quite think
Somehow his body, for instance,
Was intermittent

He could see the bread he cut
He could see the letters of words he read
He could see the wrinkles on handskin he looked at
Or one eye of a person
Or an ear, or a foot, or the other foot
But somehow he could not quite see

Nevertheless the Grand Canyon spread wide open
Like a surgical operation for him
But somehow he had only half a face there
And somehow his legs were missing at the time
And though somebody was talking he could not hear
Though luckily his camera worked O.K.
The sea-bed lifted its privacy
And showed its most hidden fish-thing
He stared he groped to feel
But his hands were funny hooves just at the crucial moment
And though his eyes worked
Half his head was jellyfish, nothing could connect
And the photographs were blurred
A great battleship broke in two with a boom
As if to welcome his glance
An earthquake shook a city onto its people

Just before he got there
With his rubber eye his clockwork ear
And the most beautiful girls
Laid their faces on his pillow staring him out
But somehow his eyes were in the wrong way round
He laughed he whispered but somehow he could not hear
He gripped and clawed but somehow his fingers would not
                                                                                catch

Somehow he was a tar-baby
Somehow somebody was pouring his brains into a bottle
Somehow he was already too late
And was a pile of pieces under a blanket
And when the seamonster surfaced and stared at the rowboat
Somehow his eyes failed to click
And when he saw the man's head cleft with a hatchet
Somehow staring blank swallowed his entire face
Just at the crucial moment
Then disgorged it again whole
As if nothing had happened

So he just went and ate what he could
And did what he could
And grabbed what he could
And saw what he could

Then sat down to write his autobiography

But somehow his arms were just bits of stick
Somehow his guts were an old watch-chain
Somehow his feet were two old postcards
Somehow his head was a broken windowpane

'I give up,' he said.   He gave up.

Creation had failed again.

Crow's Song of Himself

When God hammered Crow
He made gold
When God roasted Crow in the sun
He made diamond
When God crushed Crow under weights
He made alcohol
When God tore Crow to pieces
He made money
When God blew Crow up
He made day
When God hung Crow on a tree
He made fruit
When God buried Crow in the earth
He made man
When God tried to chop Crow in two
He made woman
When God said: 'You win, Crow,'
He made the Redeemer.

When God went off in despair
Crow stropped his beak and started in on the two thieves.

Crow Sickened

His illness was something could not vomit him up.

Unwinding the world like a ball of wool
Found the last end tied round his own finger.

Decided to get death, but whatever
Walked into his ambush
Was always his own body.

Where is this somebody who has me under?

He dived, he journeyed, challenging, climbed and with a
                                                    glare
Of hair on end finally met fear.

His eyes sealed up with shock, refusing to see.

With all his strength he struck. He felt the blow.

Horrified, he fell.

Song for a Phallus

There was a boy was Oedipus
    Stuck in his Mammy's belly
His Daddy'd walled the exit up
    He was a horrible fella
                Mamma   Mamma

You stay in there his Daddy cried
    Because a Dickybird
Has told the world when you get born
    You'll treat me like a turd
                Mamma   Mamma

His Mammy swelled and wept and swelled
    With a bang he busted out
His Daddy stropped his hacker
    When he heard that baby shout
                Mamma   Mamma

O do not chop his winkle off
    His Mammy cried with horror
Think of the joy will come of it
    Tomorrer and tomorrer
                Mamma   Mamma

But Daddy had the word from God
    He took that howling brat
He tied its legs in crooked knots
    And threw it to the cat
                Mamma   Mamma

But Oedipus he had the luck
    For when he hit the ground

He bounced up like a jackinabox
   And knocked his Daddy down
                          Mamma   **Mamma**

He hit his Daddy such a whack
   Stone dead his Daddy fell
His cry went straight to God above
   His ghost it went to Hell
                          Mamma   **Mamma**

The Dickybird came to Oedipus
   You murderous little sod
The Sphinx will bite your bollocks off
   This order comes from God
                          Mamma   **Mamma**

The Sphinx she waved her legs at him
   And opened wide her maw
Oedipus stood stiff and wept
   At the dreadful thing he saw
                          Mamma   **Mamma**

He stood there on his crooked leg
   The Sphinx began to bawl
Four legs three legs two legs one leg
   Who goes on them all
                          Mamma   **Mamma**

Oedipus took an axe and split
   The Sphinx from top to bottom
The answers aren't in me, he cried
   Maybe your guts have got em
                          Mamma   **Mamma**

And out there came ten thousand ghosts
    All in their rotten bodies
Crying, You will never know
    What a cruel bastard God is
                              Mamma   Mamma

Next came out his Daddy dead
    And shrieked about the place
He stabs his Mammy in the guts
    And smiles into her face
                              Mamma   Mamma

Then out his Mammy came herself
    The blood poured from her bucket
What you can't understand, she cried
    You sleep on it or sing to it
                              Mamma   Mamma

Oedipus raised his axe again
    The World is dark, he cried
The World is dark one inch ahead
    What's on the other side?
                              Mamma   Mamma

He split his Mammy like a melon
    He was drenched with gore
He found himself curled up inside
    As if he had never been bore
                              Mamma   Mamma

Apple Tragedy

So on the seventh day
The serpent rested.
God came up to him.
'I've invented a new game,' he said.

The serpent stared in surprise
At this interloper.
But God said: 'You see this apple?
I squeeze it and look—Cider.'

The serpent had a good drink
And curled up into a questionmark.
Adam drank and said: 'Be my god.'
Eve drank and opened her legs

And called to the cockeyed serpent
And gave him a wild time.
God ran and told Adam
Who in drunken rage tried to hang himself in the orchard.

The serpent tried to explain, crying 'Stop'
But drink was splitting his syllable
And Eve started screeching: 'Rape! Rape!'
And stamping on his head.

Now whenever the snake appears she screeches
'Here it comes again! Help! Help!'
Then Adam smashes a chair on its head,
And God says: 'I am well pleased'

And everything goes to hell.

Crow Paints Himself into a Chinese Mural

The grass camps in its tussock
With its spears and banners, at nightfall.

A ghost comes
With the circumspect ribs of a tank
Crumpled to wet cardboard
And all the crew grinning out
As out of a wedding photo
Scorched, black-edged, in wet ashes—

My thin shoesoles tremble,
And the sulphur-blast passes, the fright-glare.
And the people scamper past, coughing and stumbling.
(The picture blurred, for even the eye trembles)
The trees cough and shake,
And the great lizards go galloping past, heads high,
And horses breaking to freedom.
The soil cracks between tussock and tussock
Between my feet, as a mouth trying to speak,
The mortuary heart and guts of the globe
Trying to speak, against gravity,
The still-warm, stopped brain of a just-dead god
Trying to speak
Against its thickening death,
The mauled, blood-plastered, bodiless head of a planet
Trying to speak,
Lopped before birth
Rolled off into space, with mouth smashed
And tongue still moving
To find mother, among the stars and the blood-spittle,
Trying to cry—

And a blackbird sitting in the plum tree
Shakes and shakes its voice.

And I too am a ghost. I am the ghost
Of a great general, silent at my chess.
A million years have gone over
As I finger one piece.

The dusk waits.

The spears, the banners, wait.

Crow's Last Stand

Burning
       burning
              burning
                      there was finally something
The sun could not burn, that it had rendered
Everything down to—a final obstacle
Against which it raged and charred

And rages and chars

Limpid among the glaring furnace clinkers
The pulsing blue tongues and the red and the yellow
The green lickings of the conflagration

Limpid and black—

Crow's eye-pupil, in the tower of its scorched fort.

Crow and the Sea

He tried ignoring the sea
But it was bigger than death, just as it was bigger than life.

He tried talking to the sea
But his brain shuttered and his eyes winced from it as from
open flame.

He tried sympathy for the sea
But it shouldered him off—as a dead thing shoulders you off.

He tried hating the sea
But instantly felt like a scrutty dry rabbit-dropping on the
windy cliff.

He tried just being in the same world as the sea
But his lungs were not deep enough

And his cheery blood banged off it
Like a water-drop off a hot stove.

Finally

He turned his back and he marched away from the sea

As a crucified man cannot move.

Truth Kills Everybody

So Crow found Proteus—steaming in the sun.
Stinking with sea-bottom growths
Like the plug of the earth's sump-outlet.
There he lay—belching quakily.

Crow pounced and buried his talons—

And it was the famous bulging Achilles—but he held him
The oesophagus of a staring shark—but he held it
A wreath of lashing mambas—but he held it

It was a naked powerline, 2000 volts—
He stood aside, watching his body go blue
As he held it and held it

It was a screeching woman and he had her by the throat—
He held it

A gone steering wheel bouncing towards a cliff edge—
He held it

A trunk of jewels dragging into a black depth—he held it

The ankle of a rising, fiery angel—he held it

Christ's hot pounding heart—he held it

The earth, shrunk to the size of a hand grenade

And he held it he held it and held it and

BANG!

He was blasted to nothing.

Crow and Stone

Crow was nimble but had to be careful
Of his eyes, the two dewdrops.
Stone, champion of the globe, lumbered towards him.

No point in detailing a battle
Where stone battered itself featureless
While Crow grew perforce nimbler.

The subnormal arena of space, agog,
Cheered these gladiators many aeons.
Still their struggle resounds.

But by now the stone is a dust—flying in vain,
And Crow has become a monster—his mere eyeblink
Holding the very globe in terror.

And still he who never has been killed
Croaks helplessly
And is only just born.

Fragment of an Ancient Tablet

Above—the well-known lips, delicately downed.
Below—beard between thighs.

Above—her brow, the notable casket of gems.
Below—the belly with its blood-knot.

Above—many a painful frown.
Below—the ticking bomb of the future.

Above—her perfect teeth, with the hint of a fang at the
                                                    corner.
Below—the millstones of two worlds.

Above—a word and a sigh.
Below—gouts of blood and babies.

Above—the face, shaped like a perfect heart.
Below—the heart's torn face.

Notes for a Little Play

First—the sun coming closer, growing by the minute.
Next—clothes torn off.
Without a goodbye
Faces and eyes evaporate.
Brains evaporate.
Hands arms legs feet head and neck
Chest and belly vanish
With all the rubbish of the earth.

And the flame fills all space.
The demolition is total
Except for two strange items remaining in the flames—
Two survivors, moving in the flames blindly.

Mutations—at home in the nuclear glare.

Horrors—hairy and slobbery, glossy and raw.

They sniff towards each other in the emptiness.

They fasten together. They seem to be eating each other.

But they are not eating each other.

They do not know what else to do.

They have begun to dance a strange dance.

And this is the marriage of these simple creatures—
Celebrated here, in the darkness of the sun,

Without guest or God.

Snake Hymn

The snake in the garden
If it was not God
It was the gliding
And push of Adam's blood.

The blood in Adam's body
That slid into Eve
Was the everlasting thing
Adam swore was love.

The blood in Eve's body
That slid from her womb—
Knotted on the cross
It had no name.

Nothing else has happened.
The love that cannot die
Sheds the million faces
And skin of agony

To hang, an empty husk.
Still no suffering
Darkens the garden
Or the snake's song.

Lovesong

He loved her and she loved him
His kisses sucked out her whole past and future or tried to
He had no other appetite
She bit him she gnawed him she sucked
She wanted him complete inside her
Safe and sure forever and ever
Their little cries fluttered into the curtains

Her eyes wanted nothing to get away
Her looks nailed down his hands his wrists his elbows
He gripped her hard so that life
Should not drag her from that moment
He wanted all future to cease
He wanted to topple with his arms round her
Off that moment's brink and into nothing
Or everlasting or whatever there was
Her embrace was an immense press
To print him into her bones
His smiles were the garrets of a fairy palace
Where the real world would never come
Her smiles were spider bites
So he would lie still till she felt hungry
His words were occupying armies
Her laughs were an assassin's attempts
His looks were bullets daggers of revenge
Her glances were ghosts in the corner with horrible secrets
His whispers were whips and jackboots
Her kisses were lawyers steadily writing
His caresses were the last hooks of a castaway
Her love-tricks were the grinding of locks
And their deep cries crawled over the floors
Like an animal dragging a great trap

His promises were the surgeon's gag
Her promises took the top off his skull
She would get a brooch made of it
His vows pulled out all her sinews
He showed her how to make a love-knot
Her vows put his eyes in formalin
At the back of her secret drawer
Their screams stuck in the wall

Their heads fell apart into sleep like the two halves
Of a lopped melon, but love is hard to stop

In their entwined sleep they exchanged arms and legs
In their dreams their brains took each other hostage

In the morning they wore each other's face

Glimpse

'O leaves,' Crow sang, trembling, 'O leaves—'

The touch of a leaf's edge at his throat
Guillotined further comment.

                              Nevertheless
Speechless he continued to stare at the leaves

Through the god's head instantly substituted.

King of Carrion

His palace is of skulls.

His crown is the last splinters
Of the vessel of life.

His throne is the scaffold of bones, the hanged thing's
Rack and final stretcher.

His robe is the black of the last blood.

His kingdom is empty—

The empty world, from which the last cry
Flapped hugely, hopelessly away
Into the blindness and dumbness and deafness of the gulf

Returning, shrunk, silent

To reign over silence.

Two Eskimo Songs

I FLEEING FROM ETERNITY

Man came running faceless over earth
Eyeless and mouthless baldface he ran

He knew he trod the stone of death
He knew he was a ghost it was all he knew.

Feeling a million years under stones
He found a slug
                    but the lightning struck it
It fumed to a scorched halo on his numbed palm.

Feeling a million years under stones
He found a trout
                    but a white hot frost fell
From the exhaust of a star the fish frittered to crystals.

Feeling a million years under stones
He found a mouse
                    but a sigh of time
Breathed it to crumbs of knuckles.

He got a sharp rock he gashed holes in his face
Through the blood and pain he looked at the earth.

He gashed again deeper and through the blood and pain
He screeched at the lightning, at the frost, and at time.

Then, lying among the bones on the cemetary earth,
He saw a woman singing out of her belly.

He gave her eyes and a mouth, in exchange for the song.
She wept blood, she cried pain.

The pain and the blood were life. But the man laughed—

The song was worth it.

The woman felt cheated.

II HOW WATER BEGAN TO PLAY

Water wanted to live
It went to the sun it came weeping back
Water wanted to live
It went to the trees they burned it came weeping back
They rotted it came weeping back
Water wanted to live
It went to the flowers they crumpled it came weeping back
It wanted to live
It went to the womb it met blood
It came weeping back
It went to the womb it met knife
It came weeping back
It went to the womb it met maggot and rottenness
It came weeping back it wanted to die

It went to time it went through the stone door
It came weeping back
It went searching through all space for nothingness
It came weeping back it wanted to die

Till it had no weeping left

It lay at the bottom of all things

Utterly worn out   utterly clear

Littleblood

O littleblood, hiding from the mountains in the mountains
Wounded by stars and leaking shadow
Eating the medical earth.

O littleblood, little boneless little skinless
Ploughing with a linnet's carcase
Reaping the wind and threshing the stones.

O littleblood, drumming in a cow's skull
Dancing with a gnat's feet
With an elephant's nose with a crocodile's tail.

Grown so wise grown so terrible
Sucking death's mouldy tits.

Sit on my finger, sing in my ear, O littleblood.